I0804005

PAST & PRESENT

HANOVER AND DARTMOUTH COLLEGE

Opposite: The north side of East Wheelock Street is seen in this c. 1890 image. On the left is the Alpha Delta Phi fraternity house, erected in 1872 and razed in 1921 when the present building was constructed. Beyond is Dr. Carlton P. Frost's residence, which started out as the Georgian-styled house at the corner of North Main and West Wheelock Streets. The corresponding present image can be found on page 31. (Courtesy of Dartmouth College Special Collections.)

PAST & PRESENT

HANOVER AND DARTMOUTH COLLEGE

Frank J. Barrett Jr.

This book of images is dedicated to Henry Osgood Bly (1838–1903), the first-known photographer of the Hanover and Dartmouth environment. From Norwich, Vermont, by 1860 he had established himself as a photographer with a studio at the "Village at the College." He had an artist's eye for good composition, contrasting light and shadow and creating balance and interest in his photographs. Many of his images are reproduced in this book.

ISBN 978-1-4671-0880-5

Library of Congress Control Number: 2022938577

Published by Arcadia Publishing
Charleston, South Carolina

Printed in the United States of America

For all general information, please contact Arcadia Publishing:
Telephone 843-853-2070
Fax 843-853-0044
E-mail sales@arcadiapublishing.com
For customer service and orders:
Toll-Free 1-888-313-2665

Visit us on the Internet at www.arcadiapublishing.com

On the Front Cover: The east side of South Main Street is seen here looking toward the intersection of Wheelock and Main Streets about 1860; 122 years later, the changes in the vibrant downtown center are evident with a loss of buildings due to fire and obsolescence. (Courtesy of Dartmouth College Special Collections.)

On the Back Cover: The center of village life has from the beginning been the intersection of Wheelock and Main Streets. A.P. Balch's mansion, the "Golden Corner" (1875–1900), and the Dartmouth Savings Bank building (1870–1913) were replaced by Dartmouth's College Hall and Robinson Hall in the early years of the 20th century. (Courtesy of Dartmouth College Special Collections.)

Contents

Acknowledgments

As with my past book efforts detailing the history of Hanover and Dartmouth College, published by Arcadia and the History Press, I am grateful for the work of past historians who have carefully detailed the earlier years of the "College on the Hill" and the "Village at the College." And, too, I am grateful for the generosity of Dartmouth College Special Collections for the many superb historical images that are so integral to this present work. The present-day photographs were, for better or for worse, taken by the author while dodging traffic—something the 19th-century photographers did not need to be concerned with.

Introduction

On July 4, 1961, when Hanover held its bicentennial celebration, I was an eight-year-old boy growing up in downtown Hanover with a deep fascination for local history, buildings, and architecture. And like my father and namesake, I had by then decided that I too, just like him, wanted to be an architect with a deep appreciation of history. In those years, now a long time ago, from the seat of my bicycle, I watched buildings being moved, demolished, altered, and constructed. And, too, at an early age, I came to realize that architecture and history are inescapably interwoven as one—the stories of persons and places, triumph and tragedy, loss, defeat and progress, and the left-behind reflections, hopes, and aspirations of each passing generation. This became especially apparent to me as I learned of the history of the built environment of my hometown, because from the start, the college and village were, in reality, uniquely one, as proven by the intertwined growth and development that they shared, the tragedies suffered, and the triumphs experienced.

At the time of the bicentennial, my father purchased a copy of *Hanover, New Hampshire: A Bicentennial Book; Essays in Celebration of the Town's 200 Anniversary*, a wonderful hardcover text containing 22 chapters superbly researched and written by a committee of knowledgeable Hanover citizens. Also included in this single volume were 47 carefully reproduced old images of Hanover and Dartmouth from long ago. This book, which I still have, is now very well worn, with a failing binding and yellowing pages, but nonetheless, it occupies a proud place on my bookshelf of all things Hanover. As a youngster, I read countless times the chapter titled "The Christie Warden Murder" written by Robert P. Richmond. When I reached sixth grade at Hanover Elementary School, I was delighted that Richmond's wife, Frances, was my history teacher. And the chapter titled "Early Houses: In the Village on the Plain" by Jeannette Mather Lord was likewise almost memorized. I was especially delighted that my adolescent girlfriend at the time, Sara Scotford, lived in the two-story Aaron Hutchinson house, originally erected in 1810 on the present-day site of Steele Hall and moved in 1920 to 39 College Street. Her dad, John R. Scotford Jr., was a very talented graphic artist at Dartmouth, and with his wife, Anne, they had a deep appreciation for the house's antiquity, including the graceful original stairway in the front hall, and the abundance of original woodwork including wall dado and fireplace mantles. Lord observed that the house had lower ceilings on the first floor than on the second, and that speculation existed up to the present day that too much rum was served too early in the day when the heavy timber post-and-beam frame was raised, and it ended up being erected upside down. Because of the time spent in that house, a lot was learned by this young budding architect and historian. Since that time, the house has been moved twice; today, it is at 13 Lyme Road.

The 47 historical images contained within the book were a never-ending source of interest for me. In almost all cases, they were of buildings gone by 1961; however, continued study and fascination with their stories have caused them to become like portraits of long-ago-departed old friends and relatives. Although never experiencing these old buildings directly, to this day, I feel as though I've known them my entire life. Furthermore, it was about this time that my maternal grandmother, who we affectionately called "Nanny," gave me a small handful of old hand-colored postcards of Hanover and Dartmouth, all postmarked 1908. She was a strikingly lovely young woman coming of age in Cambridge, Massachusetts, soon to start her studies at Radcliffe College. She had a boyfriend named Alfred, who was attending Dartmouth College. After a year, the romance was over (Nanny married a Harvard man); however, she kept the postcards Alfred had sent her and about half a century later she gave them to me. My favorite was the view of South Main Street that showed the old Hanover Inn—a lovable pile of late-Victorian-era brick and sandstone torn down in June 1966. This handful of postcards became the nucleus of a vintage postcard collection that now numbers well into the many thousands and extends into the upper valley, well beyond downtown Hanover.

Since 1997, I have had the opportunity to compile and publish four books about Hanover history. That year the first such volume, simply titled *Hanover, New Hampshire*, was published by Arcadia Publishing, as part of its Images of America series. This first book dealt with the evolution of the downtown and campus area from about 1890 to 1940. Several more related volumes followed, the most recent published in 2021 by the History Press.

Because of the unique relationship of the college and downtown area to each other, coupled with the fact that from an early age the area was so well photographed, it occurred to me that it would be fun to compile a "then and now" look at the community, utilizing Arcadia's format designed exactly for that purpose. After all, one does not need to be an avid historian to enjoy such photographic comparisons. And for those wanting to know more, I reasoned that using this book together with my four previous volumes, an enjoyable understanding of the built environment could be readily had by the interested reader.

As discussed in detail within the pages of my previous *Lost Hanover* book, by the 19th century the Village at the College and the College on the Hill came to be common references to what is present-day downtown Hanover and the Dartmouth College campus. And, as touched upon above, since 1770, they have been for all intents and purposes intertwined almost as one. Therefore, this book is arranged such that it can be a walking tour of sorts of the downtown and campus area, especially if used in conjunction with my earlier Hanover-related books.

The economical and efficient format of this book only allowed for a certain number of photographs, and limited space for captains. Therefore, some hard choices had to be made as to the selection of images, both historical and present, and the amount and content of the text. Nonetheless, as in the past, thanks and acknowledgment is made to Dartmouth Collect Special Collections and the extensive historical archives available at Rauner Library, and to Arcadia editor Erin Vosgien, who once again understood the value of this effort and prompted me to undertake its compilation. It is my hope that the reader will enjoy this tour of a wonderfully vibrant and ever-changing community. As I dodged modern-day vehicular traffic with my digital camera, taking the present-day images used in this book, I could not help but smile as I envisioned Henry Osgood Bly, with his heavy wooden camera tripod set up in the middle of the intersection of Wheelock and Main Streets beside the Dartmouth Hotel, or at the corner of Lebanon Street looking north, adjacent to his studio and shop, taking his magnificent early images of the streetscape and environs of the Village at the College.

Frank J. Barrett Jr.
April 2022
Greensboro Bend, Vermont

CHAPTER 1

THE COLLEGE ON THE HILL

Dartmouth Row is seen in this c. 1870 image. Hanover resident and land surveyor Jonathan Freeman laid out the green and surrounding streets in June 1771. Upon the completion of Reed Hall in 1839 (right), it was planned that a duplicate to it would be constructed, in a symmetrical relationship, at the north end of the row, on the present-day site of Rollins Chapel. (Dartmouth College Special Collections.)

This c. 1860 view below shows the original wood-framed Dartmouth Hall (1791) with white painted clapboards; however, the brick Wentworth and Thornton Halls (1829), and Reed Hall (1839), designed by architect Ammi Burnham Young (1798–1874), remain unpainted. Dartmouth Hall tragically burned on February 18, 1904, but two years later to the day, a close duplicate, this time in brick, was dedicated and took its place. (Past image, Dartmouth College Special Collections.)

The past image of the northerly side of the green, looking west along Wentworth Street in 1854, is believed to be the oldest known photograph of Hanover. In the foreground, on the site of present-day Webster Hall and Rauner Library, is Lang Hall (1799–1865), which housed Richard Lang's general store on the first floor and a lecture hall above. (Past image, Dartmouth College Special Collections.)

The northwest corner of the green is seen in the past image as it had developed by 1867. From left to right are the Samuel McClure residence (1784); the Hubbard residence (1842); and the Crosby residence (1810). Between the Hubbard and Crosby residences, barely visible behind the trees, is the so-called "Academy Building," erected in 1837 for Moor's Indian Charity School. (Past image, Dartmouth College Special Collections.)

The north side of the green is seen as it appeared around 1875 after the removal of Lang Hall in 1865 and the addition of vestibules to the church in 1869. From left to right are Church Vestry (1841–1931), Church of Christ at Dartmouth College (1795–1931), Choate House (1786), Lord House (1802), and Rood House (1824–1900). The green was fenced in 1836, and the fencing was removed in 1893. Webster Hall, designed by architect Charles Alonso Rich, was completed in 1907. (Past image, author's collection.)

The Church of Christ at Dartmouth College, completed in 1795, evolved architecturally until its fiery destruction on the night of May 13, 1931. The original tall spire was replaced with a new belfry in 1838, and entrance vestibules were added in 1869. The building was lengthened in 1877. In 1889, New York City architect Stanford White (1853–1906) remodeled the building including a rear addition to accommodate a new pipe organ—the gift of Hiram Hitchcock in memory of his wife, Mary. (Past image, Dartmouth College Special Collections.)

The views in this and the preceding historical image were only possible between 1928, when construction of Baker Library and Sanborn House was completed, and May 13, 1931, when the church and vestry were destroyed by fire. Prior to the fire, the cause of which was never determined, Dartmouth College president Ernest Martin Hopkins had ambitions of razing Rollins Chapel and moving the venerable 136-year-old church building to the site of that then unwanted "Victorian pile of rubble." (Past image, Dartmouth College Special Collections.)

The house built in 1784 by Samuel McClure and owned for many years by Dr. Shurtleff and his family was razed in 1910 to allow construction of Parkhurst Hall. The college had acquired the property in 1900, as it was doing at that time along the entire west side of the green. Charles Alonzo Rich was the architect of Parkhurst Hall, designed in the fashionable Beaux-Arts style so favored by that generation. (Past image, Dartmouth College Special Collections.)

The 1842 Hubbard residence was acquired by the college, and in 1899, it was remodeled to become a 20-student dormitory called Hubbard Hall. In 1906, a large four-story annex was added to the rear, but all of this was short-lived. In 1910, the original front building, shown here, was razed to make way for the construction of Parkhurst Hall. The newly constructed dormitory annex was moved back, and it too was razed in 1931. (Past image, Dartmouth College Special Collections.)

Perhaps the most unfortunate building on campus, subjected to changing needs and shifts in architectural tastes, was the one designed by Ammi B. Young in 1837 for Moor's Indian Charity School. Extensively altered in 1871 for the Chandler School and then further altered and expanded in 1898, by 1937, it was an unwanted orphan considered "unquestionably the ugliest building in Hanover," and demolished. By then there was not a trace remaining of Young's original Greek Revival design. (Past image, Dartmouth College Special Collections.)

The residence built in 1810 for Rev. Dr. Zephaniah Moore was for many years owned by Prof. Dr. Dixi Crosby. Here, in 1853, Crosby made experiments evaluating Pennsylvania "rock oil," which led to the establishment of the petroleum industry. The college acquired the property in 1896 and extensively remodeled it with a large addition. In 1980, the building was again remodeled, and the old 1896 rear addition was replaced with a larger building on the back. (Past image, Dartmouth College Special Collections.)

The initial layout of the green envisioned residential development along the west side of North Main Street to support the college. This c. 1860 view from Wentworth Street looking west shows, from left to right, a portion of the 1774 Comfort Sever residence; the three-story residence of Dr. Cyrus Perkins erected in 1815, later known as Sanborn House, which replaced an earlier and more modest home; and the 1810 Prof. Ebenezer Adams residence, later known as Proctor House. (Past image, Dartmouth College Special Collections.)

The 1810 home of Professor Adams became known as Proctor House. In 1902, it was acquired by the college and moved back for construction of the new Tuck School's Tuck Hall, designed by architect Charles Alonzo Rich. The house was demolished in 1912 to make way for South Massachusetts Hall, and the original Tuck School building was substantially remodeled in 1930 by architect Jens Fredrik Larson to become McNutt Hall. The lane to the cemetery is to the left. (Past image, Dartmouth College Special Collections.)

It is unknown who designed Dr. Perkins's new house in 1815; however, by 1894, it was owned by the college and was known as Sanborn Hall. That year, a massive dormitory addition was made to the building. In 1913, it was moved back from the street, and Robinson Hall, designed by Charles Alonzo Rich, was erected. Finally, in 1936, the old Sanborn Hall was demolished to make way for Thayer Dining Hall. (Past image, Dartmouth College Special Collections.)

Not a single building visible in this 1867 view looking north along North Main Street is still extant. At far left is the 1774 Comfort Sever house, which was moved to 16 West Wheelock Street in 1870 to allow for the construction of the new Dartmouth Savings Bank building (see page 93). Beyond it is the 1815 Dr. Cyrus Perkins house, later known as Sanborn Hall. To the right is the green, the Church of Christ, and houses along Wentworth Street. (Past image, Dartmouth College Special Collections.)

Within 25 years, three buildings occupied the corner of North Main and Wheelock Streets. The c. 1867 view shows the residence built by successful Hanover merchant Richard Lang in 1795, which in 1875 was moved away. The Balch Mansion, called "the Golden Corner," was then constructed. The mansion partially burned in 1900, was bought by the college, and was demolished except for the granite front steps. That year College Hall, designed by architect Charles Alonso Rich, was built. (Past image, Dartmouth College Special Collections.)

Second Empire "French" architecture in Hanover is seen in this c. 1880 image. The Dartmouth Savings Bank (1870–1913) on the right also served as the college treasurer's office. The house erected by Adna Perkins Balch (1817–1889) in 1876 was used as a general store and fraternity house following Balch's death before partially burning in 1900. The granite front steps remain as part of College Hall. Robinson Hall was erected in 1913, designed by architect Charles Alonzo Rich. (Past image, Dartmouth College Special Collections.)

The first building erected on the south side of the green was a house for Dr. John Crane in 1773, visible in the center of this 1867 photograph. To the left is Bissell Hall (1867–1959), the new gymnasium. At far right is the brick Dartmouth Hotel (1813–1887) and the large wood-frame hotel annex building. The Crane house and hotel buildings were destroyed by "the Great Hotel Fire" of January 4, 1887. (Past image, Dartmouth College Special Collections.)

Bissell Hall, designed by architect Joseph R. Richards of Boston, was first a gymnasium before becoming the home of the Thayer School of Civil Engineering in 1910. By 1959, the building had become an unwanted orphan and was razed to make way for the four-acre redevelopment of Hopkins Center for the Arts, designed by New York architect Wallace K. Harrison (1895–1981). Opened in 1962, Hopkins Center had been in the planning stages for about 30 years. (Past image, author's collection.)

This c. 1874 image looks east from the intersection of East Wheelock and College Streets. Culver Hall (left, 1870–1929) and Conant Hall (right, 1874–1925) were owned by the State of New Hampshire and were part of the New Hampshire College of Agriculture and Mechanical Arts. In the distance is the farm on South Park Street that was part of the school. In 1893, the state college left Hanover for Durham and became the University of New Hampshire. (Past image, Dartmouth College Special Collections.)

The north side of East Wheelock Street is seen around 1890. At left is the Alpha Delta Phi fraternity house, erected in 1872 and razed in 1921 when the present building was constructed. Beyond is Dr. Carlton P. Frost's residence, which started out as the Georgian-style home at the corner of North Main and West Wheelock Streets (see page 26). In 1911, it became the Chi Phi fraternity, and was moved to South Park Street in 1927. (Past image, Dartmouth College Special Collections.)

Culver Hall (1871–1929) was designed by architect Edward Dow of Concord, New Hampshire, as a state-of-the-art science laboratory building for the New Hampshire College of Agriculture and Mechanical Arts. Dartmouth College acquired the building in 1893 when the state school was moved to Durham. The building was razed in 1929. In the background is Shattuck Observatory (1852). (Past image, Dartmouth College Special Collections.)

Conant Hall was designed by Edward Dow in 1874 as a residential and dining facility for the state school, as shown in this view taken at completion. To the right is the chimney of the gas plant (1872–1898), built to provide gas for the lights in the college buildings. Topliff dormitory was erected in 1920, and in 1925, the front portion of Conant Hall was razed. The rear portion remains is known today as Hallgarten Hall. (Past image, Dartmouth College Special Collections.)

The building erected in 1872 by Alpha Delta Phi was the first specifically designed as a fraternity house in Hanover. By 1921, the building's Italianate brick architecture was out of style, and the fraternity needed a larger facility. The old structure was razed and replaced by a new building designed in the Georgian Revival style so popular with the collegiate generation at the time and their elders. (Past image, Dartmouth College Special Collections.)

By 1875, the house erected by Richard Lang in 1795 had become an antiquated building owned by Adna P. Balch (see page 26). Unwanted, it was moved to 11 East Wheelock Street and extensively remodeled into a stylish Second Empire–style house for Dr. Frost, with a matching stable building. As was popular at the time, a third floor was added under the Mansard-style roof. In 1927, the building was moved again to 23 South Park Street. (Past image, Dartmouth College Special Collections.)

Of all major building on the Dartmouth campus, Butterfield Museum (center), erected in 1895–1896, was the shortest-lived, razed in 1926 to make way for the construction of Baker Library. To the left is the rear of Webster Hall and Rauner Library. To the right is the 1842 Abigail Dewey house, moved to 24 East Wheelock Street to be replaced by the east entrance to Baker Library, completed in 1928. (Past image, Dartmouth College Special Collections.)

The construction of Baker Library (1925–1928) required the removal of nine major structures. The house to the left, erected in 1842 by Abigail Dewey, was moved to 24 East Wheelock Street. The house to the right, erected in 1812 by James S. Brown, a saddler by trade with a shop on the premises, was also moved and placed beside it. Today, both buildings are extant. (Past image, Dartmouth College Special Collections.)

Many early buildings in the village had multiple uses and locations. Such was the case with this building on the site of Wheeler Hall. Over the years, it was a store, assembly hall, recitation rooms, chapel, a dormitory for medical students, and finally, in 1854, a private residence. About 1880, it was moved back from the street, and alterations were made; it was then moved again to Elm Street in 1904 to make way for the 98-bed Wheeler Hall dormitory. (Past image, Dartmouth College Special Collections.)

Originally built as a tavern by early Hanover settler Deacon Benoni Dewey in 1809 and for several generations used as such, by 1916, this property was owned by Sigma Alpha Epsilon fraternity. By the late 1920s, the old house was removed from the site, and a larger brick masonry fraternity house designed in the beloved Georgian Revival style took its place looking down North College Street. (Past image, Dartmouth College Special Collections.)

What was once known as Dartmouth Medical School is the fourth-oldest medical college in the country, established in 1797. By 1811, a new building for the school had been completed, which in 1871 was substantially remodeled as it appears in this late 19th century view. It was demolished in 1963. The Sherman Fairchild Physical Sciences Center was completed in 1974, and the Burke Chemistry Building followed in 1994. (Past image, Dartmouth College Special Collections.)

Little is known about this Cape-style house, probably of very late 18th century origins. In the mid-1960s, no longer used or wanted, it was destroyed in a controlled burn for fire department practice. The present-day Sudikoff Lab facility, originally developed for Mary Hitchcock Memorial Hospital's mental health programs, was completed in 1968. (Past image, Dartmouth College Special Collections.)

This c. 1900 view looks north from the intersection of College and Maynard Streets. On the right at 43 North College Street is the house constructed in 1876 by Prof. Arthur S. Hardy. By 1893, it was the home of the president of Dartmouth College, until a new facility was completed on Webster Avenue in 1926. This architecturally eclectic building was razed around 1970. (Past image, Dartmouth College Special Collections.)

Starting about 1960, what was then known as Dartmouth Medical School, together with Mary Hitchcock Memorial Hospital, underwent an unprecedented period of dramatic growth and development. By the mid-1960s, older residences along the east side of North College Street up to the intersection of North Park Street were either razed or moved. (Past image, author's collection.)

The Dewey Family of Springfield, Massachusetts, were early Hanover settlers and for generations owned the farm on the outskirts of the village adjacent to the intersection of North Park and North College Streets. By the 1960s, the Deweys were gone, as were the farmhouse and numerous farm buildings, and the land was redeveloped for the Dartmouth Medical School campus. (Past image, Dartmouth College Special Collections.)

It is estimated that Hiram Hitchcock spent about $250,000 developing a memorial to his beloved wife, Mary. Mary Hitchcock Memorial Hospital. Opened in 1893, by the 1980s the site had become built out and too congested; therefore, a new state-of-the-art Dartmouth Hitchcock Medical Center opened out of town in 1991. Dartmouth College purchased the old hospital site, and in 1995, many of the buildings were demolished. (Past image, Dartmouth College Special Collections.)

Prior to the development of Occum Pond in 1900, this area was poorly drained, unsightly marshland. The historical view looking north shows the newly created pond and the chicken coop of Charles E. Kibbie's farm (1884) at 12 Rope Ferry Road on the right and the gravel pit at 36 Occum Ridge, which in 1915 became the location of John H. Gerould's new residence. (Past image, Dartmouth College Special Collections.)

The newly created Occum Pond is seen here looking south from the top of the gravel pit at 36 Occom Road around 1900. At center is Mary Hitchcock Memorial Hospital; above it is Dartmouth Medical School. At far right is Prof. Frank A. Sherman's house at the corner of North Main and Maynard Streets. (Past image, Dartmouth College Special Collections.)

In the late 1890s, as Dartmouth College was expanding its teaching staff, the college developed the Occum Ridge neighborhood to supply new housing. This c. 1910 view looking north shows a delightful array of domestic architecture. (Past image, Dartmouth College Special Collections.)

Located on the site of the present-day west entrance to Baker Library on North Main Street was this curious early house built by Thaddeus White, of whom little is known. In 1925, the house was purchased from the college by Prof. Ernest R. Greene, who had been living there, and was moved to 38 East Wheelock Street to make way for Baker Library. (Past image, Dartmouth College Special Collections.)

This Second Empire French-style residence was erected by Prof. Henry E. Parker in 1868–1869 at 22 North Main Street. By 1894, it was in the possession of Kappa fraternity, and by 1924, it was acquired by Dartmouth College. Two years later, the out-of-style old Victorian was razed to make way for the construction of Silsby Hall, designed by Jens Fredrik Larson. (Past image, Dartmouth College Special Collections.)

Rev. Henry Fairbanks from St. Johnsbury, Vermont, professor of natural philosophy, erected this impressive Second Empire–style estate in 1864; by the 1870s, it was the home of Hiram and Mary Hitchcock. In 1912, the college purchased the residence and its sweeping grounds that extended down to the Connecticut River and began developing the Tuck Drive area of campus. The house was razed in 1920. (Past image, Dartmouth College Special Collections.)

This c. 1865 North Main Street view looks south, and the present view is from almost 165 years later. From left to right are the Thaddeus White house (built c. 1786), the Church of Christ at Dartmouth College (1795), the church's vestry building (1841), and Prof. Dr. Dixi Crosby's residence (1810). Behind the trees is the Moor's Indian Charity School Academy Building (1837). At far right is the entrance to the Fairbanks/Hitchcock estate. (Past image, Dartmouth College Special Collections.)

CHAPTER 2

THE VILLAGE AT THE COLLEGE

Hanover has had its share of devastating fires, but none more destructive and spectacular than the so-called "Great Hotel Fire." About 2:00 a.m. on the bitterly cold Tuesday morning of January 4, 1887, a fire broke out in the wood-framed annex building of the Dartmouth Hotel, and raged out of control for seven hours. Firefighting equipment from Lebanon finally brought it under control before more of the village was destroyed. (Dartmouth College Special Collections.)

On the present-day site of Wilson Hall, about 1785, Dr. Laban Gates erected a large home for his family, as shown in this c. 1865 winter scene. In 1884, the building was moved to 68 South Main Street to make way for the construction of Wilson Hall—a 130,000-volume library designed by Boston architect Samuel J.T. Thayer. The 1773 Crane house and the brick Dartmouth Hotel are at far right. (Past image, Dartmouth College Special Collections.)

This c. 1885 view looks west along East Wheelock Street. To the left is Dorrance Currier's residence, erected by Dr. John Crane in 1777, which had recently sprouted a three-story front porch. Beyond it is the brick Dartmouth Hotel and its large wooden annex. These three buildings were destroyed in the Great Hotel Fire of January 1887. To the right is A.P. Balch's Golden Corner, at the intersection of Main and Wheelock Streets, the south side of the college green. (Past image, Dartmouth College Special Collections.)

The east side of South Main Street is seen in this c. 1865 image facing south. All four of these buildings were completely destroyed in the Great Hotel Fire of 1887. Before the fire, sometime after 1877, the handsome Greek Revival–style portico was removed from the building because it was a favorite place for students to congregate, which annoyed the hotel keeper because of their noise. (Past image, Dartmouth College Special Collections.)

This c.1865 view looks north along the east side of South Main Street, prior to the 1887 Great Hotel Fire. The small single-story shop building in the foreground was enlarged, and two stories were added in 1867; in 1991, it became the home of Ledyard National Bank. Sawyer's Store beside it was razed in 1959 for additions to the Dartmouth Savings Bank. The Tontine was the name of the large four-story brick block lost in the fire. (Past image, Dartmouth College Special Collections.)

Following the 1887 fire, the college purchased the hotel property and commissioned architect Lambert Packard of St. Johnsbury, Vermont, to design a new hotel to be called the Wheelock. Opened in 1889 and extensively remodeled in 1902, the building was razed in June 1966, and the present Hanover Inn was erected in its place. (Past image, Dartmouth College Special Collections.)

Following the devastating Great Hotel Fire of 1887, the east side of South Main Street was rebuilt; however, in 1936, the two buildings to the left beside the Hanover Inn were lost to fire. The following year, the college erected the Lang Building on the site, designed by architect Jens Fredrick Larson and named for Hanover's first successful merchant. A third floor was added in the 1970s. (Past image, Dartmouth College Special Collections.)

The center building in this c. 1865 view was originally Brewster's Tavern, erected about 1782 on the site of the present-day Hanover Inn. The building was moved to the corner of South Main and Lebanon Streets in 1813 to make way for the new Dartmouth Hotel. One hundred years later, in 1913, it was demolished to make way for the construction of the Dartmouth Savings Bank. (Past image, Dartmouth College Special Collections.)

The brick residence of Maj. William Tenney, erected in 1835 on the corner of Lebanon and South Main Streets, was a commanding and substantial presence on the streetscape. In 1929, the federal government acquired the property, and the building was razed to make way for a new post office. It was designed by the US Treasury Department in Washington, DC, and completed in 1931. W.H. Trumbull of Hanover was the general contractor. (Past image, Dartmouth College Special Collections.)

The Dartmouth Savings Bank building, constructed in 1913, also housed Dartmouth National Bank. In 1938, the building was expanded with a rear addition as seen in this 1956 view. In 1959, it almost doubled in size with the acquisition of the Eastman's Drug Store property. After Dartmouth National Bank moved to its new building in 1975, the savings bank building was once again extensively remodeled in 1977. (Past image, Dartmouth College Special Collections.)

By 1964, it was determined that the post office site needed to be expanded, and the federal government acquired the 1786 so-called Heanage House for that purpose. Although the house was for sale for $1 for its removal to a new location, there were no takers, and the largely unaltered building was destroyed in April 1965. (Past image, Dartmouth College Special Collections.)

The 1785 Dr. Laban Gates house was moved in 1884 from the site of Wilson Hall to 68 South Main Street, and until it was razed in 2007, it served as a boarding and apartment house and also housed numerous commercial tenants, as seen here in October 1960. The new brick building for Eastman's Drug Store, designed by architect Stanley Orcutt, was erected a year earlier. (Past image, author's collection.)

What started life as a large mid-19th century farmhouse on South Main Street for the sprawling Currier Farm that stretched to Lebanon Street and up Sand Hill became the Green Lantern Inn by the time of this early 1960s view. The building was razed in early 1973, and in 1985, the so-called Galleria commercial building was developed on the site. (Past image, author's collection.)

This 1902 view shows, from left to right, the first Bridgeman Block, erected in 1900 and burned on October 30, 1906, and the first half of the Davison Building, constructed in 1893. In 1903, the old Cobb's Store building was razed and replaced by the second half of the Davison Block. Dr. Samuel Alden's 1823 brick house was acquired by the Casque & Gauntlet Society in 1893. Note the two-tier watering trough for horses and dogs. (Past image, Dartmouth College Special Collections.)

Deacon Sylvester constructed the early building at left as a shoe shop and included M.M. Amaral's barbershop. Merchant Frank W. Davison took it down in 1893 for the first half of the Davison Building. In 1903, Davison razed Cobb's Store, erected about 1793, and built the second half of his business block. The property remained owned by the Davison family until 2021. The historical image was taken about 1860. (Past image, Dartmouth College Special Collections.)

Not a single building visible in this 1865 view looking north along the west side of South Main Street is extant today. In the foreground is H.O. Bly's photo gallery in the small building erected about 1800 by Prof. John Smith to house his Hanover Bookstore. Smith was also the college librarian. The building was moved to Lebanon Street in 1869. Beside it is the site of the Musgrove Building, constructed in 1915. (Past image, Dartmouth College Special Collections.)

The Episcopal Church constructed a new rectory in 1869, and two years later, in 1871, a new chapel on the left rear of the lot. The Town of Hanover redeveloped the lot with a new municipal building in 1928 designed by Larson & Wells Architects. The house was moved back and razed in 1959 to make room for parking. The chapel was moved to Currier Street, converted to a house, and razed in 2007 as part of the college's South Block development. (Past image, Dartmouth College Special Collections.)

Around 1920, a single-story retail addition was constructed across the front of the older 19th-century home that had turned into a rooming house, and by the 1960s had become decidedly run down. The Hanover Improvement Society acquired the property, and in 1969 razed the old structures and constructed the Nugget Arcade building, completed in 1970. Frank J. Barrett was the architect. (Past image, author's collection.)

What was at times known as Union House, American House, Lower Hotel, and finally a dormitory known as South Hall was destroyed by fire on July 11, 1888, along with the house shown to the right in this 1865 view. The Nugget Theater was developed by the Hanover Improvement Society and opened in 1951. The architect was Stanley W. Orcutt. (Past image, Dartmouth College Special Collections.)

This view of South Main Street looks north in 1900. Following the fire of 1888, local entrepreneur Dorrance B. Currier developed the Tavern Block at left. Never a strong commercial success, by 1957, the property had become run down and the Hanover Improvement Society, which owned the building, had it razed. From then until 1973, when the Dartmouth National Bank began construction on its new building (still extant), the site was a parking lot. To the left is the Heanage House. (Past image, Dartmouth College Special Collections.)

In 1935, Gulf Oil constructed this large Colonial Revival–style facility to service and store automobiles, known for many years as Manchester's Gulf Service Station. The building proved to be short-lived and was razed in 1963 for a new Gulf service station which, enlarged several times since then, is now a convenience store. (Past image, author's collection.)

On September 21, 1938, when the Great New England hurricane moved up the Connecticut River Valley, Hanover got hit hard with strong winds that toppled many trees in both the village area and beyond. This view looking east on Maple Street toward South Main Street shows the mess left behind. In the distance is the Tavern Block. The parking platform was built in 1973–1974, and the Dartmouth National Bank Building was erected in 1973–1975. (Past image, Dartmouth College Special Collections.)

During the summer of 1940, South Main Street was realigned and rebuilt from the intersection of Maple and South Streets to the Lebanon town line. The historical postcard image was captured around 1910, looking south from the brow of the hill. The cottage to the right was razed in the 1970s. (Past image, author's collection.)

This 1956 view of Lebanon Street looking west toward South Main Street is from a time when, as per the lettering on the door of the truck, the Precinct of Hanover ran a pig farm out on Route 120 (Lebanon Street) and picked up all village and campus household and commercial garbage for free, to feed the pigs. The operation ceased in the late 1960s, and the site was redeveloped for Trumbull-Nelson Construction Company's yard and operations office. (Past image, author's collection.)

Hardly recognizable today is this 1956 view of the north side of Lebanon Street, taken from the loading dock driveway of the Dartmouth Ski manufacturing building. The small building at right center was a commercial laundry. The Dartmouth Savings Bank (left) was enlarged in 1959, and all of the wood-frame buildings (center and right) were razed that year for the construction of the Hopkins Center, completed in the fall of 1962. (Past image, author's collection.)

This 1956 image shows, from left to right, Trumbull-Nelson Construction Company's offices and carpentry shop, Hanover Hardware Company's paint store, the Hanover Diner, and the buildings owned by Dartmouth Ski. The Hanover Park building was completed in 1990, and the building at 11 Lebanon Street was completed about 1999. The parking lot and building in the foreground were part of the Hopkins Center redevelopment that started in 1959. (Past image, author's collection.)

Starting with the initial street layout in the village and college area, there were two College Streets: North and South. The division line was East Wheelock Street. In 1959, when construction was begun for Hopkins Center, South College Street, running between East Wheelock and Lebanon Streets, ceased to exist. This 1956 view, looking north up South College Street, shows the east and back side of Bissell Hall beyond, which was also razed in 1959. (Past image, author's collection.)

South Hall was one of 14 buildings cleared in 1959 from the four-acre site that became Hopkins Center. This c. 1925 view shows the building once located at the northeast corner of Lebanon and South College Streets. The rear portion started life in 1841 as a Methodist church, and by 1887, the front portion had been added as a hotel and the former church was turned into an opera house. (Past image, Dartmouth College Special Collections.)

Until moving to the newly completed New Hampshire Route 120 in Lebanon in 1966 and becoming Hill Crest Motors, Roger's Garage, a Chevrolet and Packard dealership, was owned and operated by F. Manning Moody on land leased from Dartmouth College. This view, taken in the fall of 1956, shows the showroom designed by Wells & Hudson Architects in 1931. The front building was razed in 1966. The site and remaining buildings were redeveloped in 2012 as the Black Family Visual Arts Center. (Past image, author's collection.)

This c. 1890 image looking west up Lebanon Street shows the brick house to the left constructed about 1840 by Methodist minister John Williams. In 1962, the two houses beyond it were razed and the Hanover Inn Motor Lodge took their place. Designed by architect W. Brooke Fleck, today the building is known as The Lodge, a dormitory for Dartmouth students. Beyond it is the Grange Building. (Past image, Dartmouth College Special Collections.)

Dartmouth College's first Sachem Village, 24 duplex buildings of married student housing, was developed on Lebanon Street in 1946–1947, following World War II. At that time, Hovey Lane ran between the housing complex and the elementary school. In 1958, all 24 units were moved one at a time, on a specially built trailer, to the newly developed second Sachem Village in West Lebanon. The site became playground space for the school. Hovey Lane was relocated in the early 1960s. (Past image, Dartmouth College Special Collections.)

Since about the 1920s, at least three service station buildings have occupied the present CO-OP site at the intersection of South Park and Lebanon Streets. As illustrated by this c. 1960 view, they followed popular architectural tastes of the time, including sleek Art Moderne styling. By about 1970, this second building was replaced with something becoming more favored: a new building rusticated with brick, a gabled roof, and dark trim. (Past image, author's collection.)

The fiery explosion in the early morning of Friday, January 28, 1944, that wrecked the Nugget Theater caused wartime movie watching to be moved to Webster Hall, and the front lobby area was salvaged and made into a Western Union telegraph office, as seen here around 1965. In 1968 the building was razed, and the site became the location of the Banwell Building and the offices of Banwell, White & Arnold Architects. (Past image, Dartmouth College Special Collections.)

The first frame building erected in 1771 was in front of the present-day Casque & Gauntlet Society—a tavern operated by Aaron Storrs. In 1823, the building was moved to West Wheelock Street, and in 1908, it became Delta Kappa Epsilon fraternity and was heavily altered to be almost unrecognizable. By 1974, owned by the Town of Hanover, the building had become quite decrepit and was razed. The site remains a parking lot. (Past image, Dartmouth College Special Collections.)

Many of the first generation of fraternity houses started life as single-family village homes, as was the case with this residence erected about 1840. By 1907, it became the Phi Gamma Delta fraternity and was embellished with columns salvaged from Cobb's Store on South Main Street when it was taken down in 1903. The present building, designed by architect Alfred Hoyt Granger of Chicago, was constructed in 1937 and replaced the earlier building. (Past image, Dartmouth College Special Collections.)

Probably as grand a house as built in the village in the early years of the 19th century was this Greek Revival–style residence of Stephen Brown, erected in 1835. Little is now known about Brown; however, since about 1902, the property has been the home of several Dartmouth fraternities with numerous additions and alterations. (Past image, Dartmouth College Special Collections.)

Following the relocation of both the elementary and high schools to Lebanon Street by 1936, the former elementary school building, erected in 1877 and expanded in 1896, was razed and the property was redeveloped by W.H. Trumbull into three residential house sites. This historical view shows the building shortly before its demolition—unused, unwanted, and painfully out of style. (Past image, author's collection.)

Coming from the railroad station in Lewiston and ascending the West Wheelock Street hill for the first time, this may well have been the first view of the Dartmouth campus seen by a first-year student around 1880. Village wags referred to the Balch mansion, erected in 1875, as the Golden Corner, and after it partially burned in 1900, the property was acquired by Dartmouth, and College Hall was constructed. (Past image, Dartmouth College Special Collections.)

Architect Frederick Clarke Withers (1828–1901) of New York City was well known for the design of churches in the English Gothic Revival style. Before the construction of St. Thomas Episcopal Church could be completed in 1876, funds had run out, eliminating the planned 150-foot stone tower. In 1958, architect Frank J. Barrett designed the stone narthex that completed the building. (Past image, Dartmouth College Special Collections.)

Perched at the brow of the West Wheelock Street hill was the residence erected in 1820 by Col. Amos A. Brewster, who developed the Dartmouth Hotel on the present site of the Hanover Inn (1813–1887). In later years, it was owned by Dartmouth College president Asa D. Smith. The building was heavily altered, and by the mid-20th century, it was demolished. (Past image, Dartmouth College Special Collections.)

One of the village's earliest houses was erected on North Main Street in 1774 by Comfort Seaver, a carpenter from Stillwater, New York (see page 25). In 1870, it was moved to West Wheelock Street to make way for the construction of the new Dartmouth Savings Bank and remained a largely unaltered single-family residence until being torn down in the mid-1980s and replaced by a complex of townhouses. (Past image, author's collection.)

This c. 1865 view from the brow of the West Wheelock Street hill looks toward Vermont. In earlier years, the street was little more than a steep and crude cart road cutting up through an eroding ravine. When Ledyard Bridge was replaced around 1999, the street was extensively rebuilt, and an attempt was made to lessen the grade, especially at the top. (Past image, Dartmouth College Special Collections.)

The Connecticut & Passumpsic Rivers Railroad opened for business in October 1848 and became Hanover's new gateway to the outside world. In the center of this late 19th century view is the railroad station, set within the busy village of Lewiston. The first Ledyard Bridge (1859–1934) is in the foreground. The road and bridge assumed their current realignment during the construction of the third and present Ledyard Bridge, finished in 2000. (Past image, Dartmouth College Special Collections.)

Consistent with our mission to preserve history on a local level, this book was printed in South Carolina on American-made paper and manufactured entirely in the United States. Products carrying the accredited Forest Stewardship Council (FSC) label are printed on 100 percent FSC-certified paper.

MADE IN THE USA